From a Mobile Home

NUALA ARCHER

From a Mobile Home

SALMON POETRY

Published in 1995 by
Salmon Publishing Ltd,
Upper Fairhill, Galway

The Publishers gratefully acknowledge the support of The Arts Council.

A catalogue record for this book is available from the British Library.

ISBN 1 897648 59 6

Cover painting by Nuala Archer
The design of the Sheela-na-gig was based on an illustration from the Millenium poster "The Spirit of Women" designed by Cathleen O'Neill with illustrations by Marina Forrestal, reprinted by permission of Attic Press.
Cover design by Poolbeg Group Services Ltd
Set by Thaddeus Root & Poolbeg Group Services Ltd in Goudy
Printed by Colour Books, Baldoyle Industrial Estate, Dublin 13.

BY NUALA ARCHER

Whale On The Line
Two Women, Two Shores
Pan / amá (Chapbook)
The Hour of Pan / amá

Grateful acknowledgement is due to the following periodicals and books in which some poems have previously appeared: American Poetry Review, "From a Mobile Home: See You in Electra"; Biodegradable News, "Wild Turkeys at Vinson"; Berkeley Poetry Review, "From a Mobile Home: Splashie Sweeping"; Calyx, "She Had Licked Her Name"; Colorado State Review, "Train Trance: Paper City"; Cream City Review, "Between Swilly and Sewanee," "Star*Mapping My Trans*atlantic Com*mutes"; Cyphers, "From a Mobile Home: Kickin' Ass Quietly," "The Wing of an Ordinary Dragonfly"; The Juke Joint Journal, "From a Mobile Home: Kickin' Ass Quietly"; Land/4, (Paris, France), "Three Woven Threads"; Land/5-6, (Paris, France), "Late Night Reading"; Maryland Poetry Review, "A Breaking, A Bread-Colored Light," "The Wing of an Ordinary Dragonfly"; Mid-American Review, "From a Mobile Home: Black Mesa Rendezvous"; Midland Review, "Brown Electric Blanket," "From a Mobile Home: Kickin' Ass Quietly," "Red Mud Music"; Nimrod, "In Bright Gray and Lavender Fissures," "Here in Oklahoma"; North Dakota Quarterly, "From a Mobile Home: Bohemian Waxwings"; The Oklahoma Observer, "Lady Liberty Talks"; Pequod, "Pear Tree & Prophecy"; Piecework, "From a Mobile Home: Self-Portrait at 31," "From a Mobile Home: Red Mud Music"; Poetry Australia, "The Scalds"; Poetry Ireland Review #41, "Sheela^Na^Gigging Around"; Portland Review Magazine, "From a Mobile Home: See You in Electra"; The Phoenix, "A Breaking, A Bread-Colored Light"; renegade, "Lady Liberty Talks"; Rubicon, "Wild Turkeys at Vinson," "Delirium of Destination"; Seneca Review, "From a Mobile Home: Through the Os of Booger Holler"; Visions International, "Edge Skool," "Giant Irish Deer"; Westview, "From a Mobile Home: First Rattler"; Widener Review, "From a Mobile Home: Azoozal Love."

"A Breaking, A Bread-Colored Light," "Bewteen Swilly and Sewanee," "Train Trance," "Brown Electric Blanket," UNLACING: TEN IRISH-AMERICAN WOMEN POETS. Ed. by Patricia Monaghan. Fairbanks, AK.: Fireweed Press, 1987.

Some of these poems were also included in TWO WOMEN, TWO SHORES: Poems by Medbh McGuckian and Nuala Archer. Baltimore: New Poets Series and Galway: Salmon Publishing, 1989.

"Edge Skool," "Nosebleed Portrait Series: Plague of Inc.'est," THE NEXT PARISH OVER. Ed. by Patricia Monaghan: New Rivers Press, 1993.

"Sheela^Na^Gigging Around" will appear as an experimental video poem produced by Monica Pombo, funded by an Ohio Arts Council grant, 1994.

For their support, inspiration, and friendship I wish to thank Gloria Anzaldúa, Talya Birkhahn, Eavan Boland, John Brandenburg, Charlotte DeClue, Mary Dorcey, Margaret Ewing, Elizabeth Freund, Tess Gallagher, Nancy George, Judy Grahn, Vicki Green, Marilyn Hacker, Geoffrey Hartman, Mary Lydon-Hill, Jill Holmes, June Jordan, Hugh Kennedy, Martha Kennedy, Mary N. Kennedy, Jessie Lendennie, Victor Luftig, Audre Lorde, Janet Lubeski, Medbh McGuckian, Alicia Ostriker, Lisa Pelligree, Ken Pobo, Minnie Bruce Pratt, Thaddeus Root, Muriel Rukeyser, Mary Kay Ruvolo, Richard Selzer, Gertrude Stein, Ruth Stone, Monique Wittig, Martha Woodmansee.

Contents

The Wing of an Ordinary Dragonfly

Sheela^Na^Gigging Around

Sheela^Na^Gigging Around

59

Red Mud Music

The Wing of an Ordinary
Dragonfly

The Wing of an Ordinary Dragonfly

—With thanks to Naomi & Leslie Archer

The first dragonfly of spring hovered,
        then leapt into air. It darted
                among trees sweeping around the pond
                        in Stephen's Green. Inverted images
                wrinkled in the water & were framed
        in the dragonfly's transparent wings.
Each wing moved quickly forward & away,
                        briefly holding blue & green prisms.

The sun, filtering lungs of leaves
        unbuttoned me. I lay on the warm grass
                & closed my eyes. Who were all these
                        people clicking past as if in glass
                corridors? And the children—chasing sailboats,
        feeding ducks, sending vowels ballooning into
air like colored dots of silence. Zero-shaped
                        sounds & eggs everywhere bursting.
In any pinch of the pond's muck: millions,
        invisible, eye-shaped eggs with life drowsing

                or waking. I drifted into a doze. A map
                        was moving under me. Directions, drunk
                as fiddlers, knocked into each other. Every
        place I'd ever lived shifted in & out of egg-
shapes. In Texas or in Tennessee my mother
                        was thinking of me here in Dublin.
And before me. Of herself. Here. A medical student
        on the Green. Then & now, dragonflies

& ducks gliding through noon's brief lunch-
            break. Air's vacancy glittering 'round
        us. Wind worrying the waters. And Mrs. O'Grady
    waiting. Suffering from a lump the size
of a small orange. Her abdomen needed listening to.
                    More than likely she needed another life.
Or just a few hours here, across the street,
        to watch lazy water fill with wings.

"

        This afternoon four yellow cranes migrated
                up O'Connell Street & are well nested among
        the deep red brick of Summerhill.
    A group of us gather as if to say good-bye
or to watch a liner going under. For years now
                    the flats have stood vacant.
The buildings shadow our way home.

        Most of us have spent a Sunday afternoon
                or more exploring the maze of rooms. These are
                    the Passage Graves of the Inner City.
                Short passages lead into larger central chambers.
        The entrance ways are decorated with patterns
as distinctive as the chevron & lozenge
                    picked in the stone along the Boyne. Here,
there are the usual face-motifs, spirals, zig-zags,
        triangles & circles as well as the madly
                flying saucers & invading Martians. Ogham-like
    lists of names are everywhere: Sandra + Paddy,
Anna + Thomas, Pauline + Pat, Marie + Sleepy.
                    Even the highest corners are initialed.

16

Names beneath names & then what?
     A palimpsest of papered walls which the wind
        is excavating. At night the children wander
          with their dogs through walls soft as Confirmation
        cake. Instinctively, with the bones
of old prams & falling roofs, they do what
has always been done. They build a bonfire, a small
           candle for the city, & from the curb
across the street, they watch the beams & buggies flame.

     Now here they are nuzzling the third story:
        the cranes. In slow-motion the heavy iron
          balls swing back, then float into the walls
        & chimneys. Girders & cement crumble
like clay cooking pots in a cloud of dust.
Nobody tells Mick to stop throwing his white mouse
        into the air as he watches. Nobody
tries to stop the pigeons from flying
     among the falling rubble. Nobody, I think, noticed
        the dragonflies surfing on top of one another
          through the last window just as it teetered
       out of place & sank to the street below.

§§§

I   am   cycling   through   the   streets
of   Summerhill.   The   only   map that makes
            sense is the wing of an ordinary dragonfly.
Familiar landmarks   are   accumulating
            to   dust.   I   am   lost.
            This   is where   they   made rounds
                together.   Here: my   mother   &
        father   in   maieutic   medical   days.
    Three-quarters   the   way   up
the   dragonfly's   wing.   At   an   intersection
                of   invisible   veins
that   eventually   forms   a   hexagon
        dazzled   by   sunlight.   From   the   zero
        of   eggs   so   many   Summerhill babies
            born   into   this   corner   of   wing.
    I   am   cycling   within   this   wing,
        this   ancient   network   of   whispers,
this   maze   of   mirrors   called   a   map.
            I   am   cycling   through   Summerhill.
And   the   walls   no   longer   walls
    no   longer   here   are   cycling   through
        me.   The   houses   fallen   to dust weave
            whispering   stories   which   circle
        the   Rotunda's   Dome   &   the   cradle
        of   grass   in   Stephen's   Green
where   I   am
    drifting   back
to   this   river's
    stuttering   &   to
        the   names   of   Summerhill
        &   to   the   houses   shining
    in   the   mosaic,   apple-green   wing
    of   an   ordinary   dragonfly
whose   veins   are   where
            I   cycle   &   the   only   sensible   map.

18

Delirium of Destinations

—For Muriel Rukeyser

Rain is painting the stones
    & who is it flying
                across the world multiplying
half-a-million by the innumerable
          quartz calculations of being alone
     among the reeks of MacGillicuddy
the soft water rocks
        of MacGillicuddy, the drowned faces,
    the invisible sun brushes
fine as the two shrimp whiskers sticking
        from your mouth &
             you an astronaut among
goat-haunted clouds?

    Why should the Khyber Pass
rise up here
            & you licking another letter
(in our mother's day the ha'-
       penny green of a monk
    at table,   reading a big book
sitting in the swerve
     of the Gaelic **E** for you-
   know-what-ewe-shaped island):
& in our own day the *salix hibernica,*

         29p, budding, flashing, cuts of Water-
            ford glass, witty
   slashes of red & blue paint
painted on sheeps' bottoms
        scattering the hillsides, & you
laughing, not ignorant of the loathing—

        & the loafing mountains
      lingering, then crowding into the dark
thunder of a Guinness: fine black
        thickness, bitter beginning,
            a donkey's kicking at the fence.
    Beside me, you kissing me
& we are dancing: "a fir-
           kin, a feather, a wild & puckish
weather" in the silent
        scented rooms dove-grey & darker of
    these mountains wet with flowers
& sky-wetness. And a great stir
      of fog is stirring the flames
  of gold-threaded turf: ferns
& fiber of a chocolate bog,
       soft fuel bed.

    There!   You speak
& word answers to word
         thing to thing, singing to singing,
Mary to Magdalene,
        The Peak of the Sheep,
    the five peaks of Cruach, the Reek,
the Cliff of the Crows,
       Bold Yellow Hill, Windy Gap
  & last, behind
the Hag's Glenn & Devil's
       Ladder, Cliff of the Goats.
          There! The hot sun
finding everything drenched,
    drowned, finding
your hay-coloured hair spread
         over the **E**—e's
of the country, & you awakening, insin-
      uating glee between gold & our throats.

Three Woven Threads

kill (U.S. dial.) n. a stream, brook:
a river: a channel
—Chambers 20th Century Dictionary

~

She asks which way

to kill & heads

for a rising

river to find

the kill is to

be met by the

momentum of

a flood to be

lost in a land

sliding where homes

let loose their beds

where centuries

slip into the

salt mouth of the

kill

≫≪

The way to kill

is just inside

the box

where mother keeps

the dried-out cords

of all

her children. *Your kill*

she said *I shall*

fly in the wind—

a red & purple flag

≫≪

To kill: I am

within

that monthly

flowering of

deconstruction,

the raining

of my occult

Punt

The Mysterious Land
of Punt Margaret Murray
says is usually dismissed

as being vaguely somewhere
on the Red Sea but if as
I suppose Punt was a generic

word for *trading station*
then the field of inquiry
is greatly enlarged if Punt merely means

trading port no matter
where situated the variety

of costumes worn by the
Punties is explained along

with the very miscellaneous ob-
jects marked MADE IN PUNT

the root of the word is PWN
the T being the usual feminine

ending for a
foreign country

Star*Mapping My Trans*Atlantic Commutes

I'm going to Ire*land a*gain

to Ire*

land a*gain   to I*

re*

land   a*

gain   cros*

sing the At*lan*tick

depress*ions

(the bat*ter*ings   the ab*

andonments)

the cri*

sis

of   this   com*

mute

this   e*

merge*

ncy long*ing

now fin*ally

for a for*

getting fin*

ally after so rig*orous

a rut of re*membering

a rain so re*

morseless

I'm going

to Ire*land ag*ai*n

to say good*bye &

hel*

lo green knives

Ire*l*a*n*d* you have cut me O*

pen into A*

wa*

ken*

ing

Nosebleed

1.
Commitment
& coils of silence
burn to the center
like insect repellent:

We love this son
who sleeps with his mother
in the grave
who I hold like a heart
to my ear
who hugs me in the dark
& wraps
the herbal scent
of my freshly shampooed hair
around his face
as he kisses you:

No wonder your nose bleeds
as we watch
incredulously
a box of yellow Kleenex
wadded to roses
collapse
in a clumsy mess,
a blood-heavy bouquet
saturated,
unstaunching.

2.
Your Florence Nightingale
for a moment
we witness me
hurl a chair
from over my head.
We leave the smithereens
of that skeleton on
the carpet of the Graduates'
Common Room
& head outside
through rain
across cobbled stones.

3.
We didn't sleep
that night. That night
we didn't touch.
The next day I left
for Paris & Pamplona.
On the boat
from Rosslair to LeHavre
I drank until I had heaved
the pearly sea of my father
out of my guts.
I drank to the dead-
center of my dread,
into my deepest denial
toward a long avoided
mourning.

I drank
until I would drink
no more
until I could touch
that starfish
hacked into a nightmare
of reproduction: incest
thriving from every lopped
limb. I connected
my terror with these
distant, untouchable
twinklings.

Edge Skool

I knew it was

dangerous going

back to the island

left behind

flying forward

into past fire

pissed families

prayers & potatoes

I sensed

at this scene

of gendering such

violence such traps

of silence &

furious hospitality

& a sacred veil

putting all in

check a crux

of codes

tongue for

tongue

So much resentment

could only have

accumulated

very slowly

year by year

day by day

century by century

the way our fathers

& Father Ireland

showered blows (but

don't you dare

tell) on

us—his disappeared

children

Swinging On A Red Gate

The dark-haired girl

on Mt. Pleasant, off

Oxford Road, swings

on a red gate

against the orange sky

cutting a spiral

through the green dome

of Rathmines Cathedral.

The red gate & dark-haired

girl shine with an inner

diamond. Mt. Pleasant's

lassitude ignites

to a vibrant indigo.

Munster & I

Must we admit hatred

here on this leaf-dappled

page of summer light

If aloud

what part in health

what's left of home

already hanging

in thinnest skeins of

almost inaccessible hope

Escalations Toward War

1.

At first there were
        homes & buildings
built in the way we are
        used to seeing them.

Then, people were running
        inside
using windows as doors
        & doors as shields.

Everyone was running because
        men were shooting
& a woman was rising
        out of a casket.

2.

Next,   was a land of   mountains
&   beneath   the mountains
a land of   boundaries   made from
tree stumps. Between   the boundaries

were   many   small   spaces.
Women   with   white
hankerchiefs   over   their eyes
lived   here.

A woman   close   to me
had   managed   to pull
the   handkerchief   above
one   of   her   eyes.

And   in   a   corner   a raven
brought   a   caged   raven
a   gift
in   her   beak

3.

A woman was swimming away
from a man who was
to her a pin-striped suit,
mustache & tie.

In front of the man--
reclining in an Easyboy--
a stand without a microphone.
On his left

a lighthouse
surrounded by a column of water.
The water continuously fell
& flowed despite him.

4.

The man was thinking:
"For the most part, it is
true—people are only lines
with here & there squares
& triangles
of sinew & nerve.
Their heads are tuna cans."

5

As the woman swam over
the horizon she realized her face—
once a caterpillar struggling
beyond the pupa stage.
Flashbacks
of insects left small legs
twitching in her mouth.
She continued swimming.
The mauve island was in sight.
She could hear the color
exchanges underway.

Train Trance: Paper City

That they blow down our streets,
can be found in all rivers,

& like kites, re-leaf the winter
trees, is by now a cliché.

Wind from the sea turns a page.
Print, like butterfly dust, powders

our fingers. But there is more
than meets the headlines.

The tangerine tree beginning to
fruit (6th edition) is a gracious

corollary to the moment just
after this photograph: the girl,

dot-to-dot, imaged here, in the rub-
ble of Summerhill, is caught on

film. Click. Click. I descend
from the commuter's track. Black

my whorls and mazes with the rub-
off inky alphabet, the scarecrow bits

of news, the transfer of her name.
I hear the glass the girl lets fly.

The splinter in my eye. Rubbish!
The vandalism of breaking light.

A Breaking, A Bread-Colored Light

Then Anne who is also
Ruth, & Nuala who
is also Miriam, came to me
as I lay curled in the ear
of a seashell. And Anne,
also Ruth, unlaced
my shoes & let them slip
to the sand of the black sea-
bed. She cradled &
kissed each step of my tired
feet while Nuala,
also Miriam, tenderly ran
her fingers through my hair
like a lover
calming my roots, combing
my broken ends.

        And to their
coming I called back: "You
are my two girls. My always-
&-for-never two girls. Ruth
also Miriam. And Nuala, also
Anne." And they lifted me up
then to the high boats
of their silence, their
beautiful bodies, & in
the boats of their bones, into
the breaking, bread-colored
light, we set sail, we broke
free, we gave thanks.

The Pear Tree & Prophecy

The pear tree, plump
a few weeks
ago with lion-colored
pears, paws,
abstractly,
the daisied grass
with its leaves
& jay-pecked fruit.

Its branches, skinny,
debouched
of their Buddhas,
are bare.
The pear tree waits
for nothing.
Waits to wait.
Expects no
saffron-dawn-glory
& accepts it
when
like today
it comes.

The pear tree
always
unprepared is ready.

From underneath
its branches
comes Prophecy
the wild, white cat

with huge eyes—
one yellow,
the other, bright
blue.
Prophecy sniffs
out the sound
of this typing
which to her means milk,
soon,
in the saucer,
& to me,
snow, soon,
on the pear tree.

Emigrant

A migrant
I know return

is impossible
the sea sieves

our unmakings
no place

can center such
only the whole

earth can vibrate
to such vagrancies

of home such reaches
of abandonment

released into
our evolving names

I now live out
the longings of this

century
the astonishing

communing
through us

Ordinary Dragonfly Flicks

Another year of dragonflies.
A drop in the bucket for these fairies
surviving 300 million years.

An early one there—hovering

Now leaping into air
Un-Stephening the Green

Framing in the minute windows
of her wings the topsy-turvy
water-wrinkled trees

like some far-out flick

featuring jazzy celluloids of turquoise & jade
with a *da capo* feminine ending—

unstressed & ongoing—

hovering among the uncertain sound tracks
of children sending vowels
ballooning into air like colored dots of silence

where pixilated directions drift
into each other & spark off lightning—

purple & pink—over a disco lake
of memory & through

a flower wilderness
a fierce unfathered woman

palpating noon's brief lunch break
transfusing its pale shadows
& razored rainbows

with her own hieroglyphic

holograms
beaming her into a body

of profound balance
merging with the laughter
& singing voices

coming from the loo labelled *mna*

Dublin Dream #2001

Beyond the fragrance

of ripening

sugarcane a road

snakes up through a

dense tropical rain forest

pulsing with blue

butterflies in a crack

of inspired memory

the road breaks

into the light of

grazing cattle & kangaroo

on a high plateau

Kookaburras

trill a pink dawn

mosquitoes are biting

where the bridge crosses

the Uiloa I open

a box a platypus

crawls out blinks

then splashes

into the vernacular

of her reedy niche

Platypus

Her collage

is a kind

of combustion

a kind of

Pegasus

she knows

there's no reason

for a horse

not to flash

with the wings

of a phoenix &

for a phoenix not

to be reborn

in the heart of this

platypus

Giant Irish Deer

I know those days

when light goes weird &

I am lifted

from gravity

to see the giant Irish

deer still grazing on

the grass that now

is called Grafton Street.

Shimmering,

translucent,

the deer slope toward

the Liffey.

Their antlers,

estuaries,

feed the dark

waters

light.

To Live Through One More
Airport Leave-Taking

Against the winter window mossy
snow multiplies the soft red warmth

& chatter. The last late dance
concentrates dawn's Etruscan slips

into each flower growing in the
gaps. What kind of language is

this, lingering even as the plane
leaves America again as the stranger's

smile lingers over our moment
of parting? Lingers even as you're

coming back to life, leaving me to linger.

Between Swilly & Sewanee

— for Naomi

Who is the mother of these words? Nonsense syllables
leaping up between Swilly & Sewanee. Three-
thousand miles of ocean: *O, bring back, bring*

back: Lovers crossing over: winging the never-
forever gap, the Atlantic assemblage: her mother
& my mother & myself: *Make me as I am—*

make me beautiful. Each with the wind of watery
trees in our faces & faith in the following dolphins—
bowing & breathing in dawn's opal brilliance,

the colostrum of our comings. Barking like Blueticks
for the sun, curling into the Q.E. II the dolphins are
the clouds at my window, nuzzling the green stillness

of flight, as if the third leave-taking were a coda,
another Rosetta story finally cracked. In the wavering
hyphens—a home between homes—a liquid blossoming

of bones—a zany confluence: the Darién & Dublin—
made flesh in a matinée of sheer quiet. Pine & palm tracks
merging. A life glowing in mots of otherly swayings.

Late Night Reading:
Multiple Exposures

Brown

brick

Ballybough

mixes strangely

with the onion transparency

& purple

of bougainvillaea

& the tides

of Panamá

impressing

expressing

the moan

of ships docked

in the Liffey's mouth

on New Year's day

Night Shift

Unemployed the sunflower in

the purple horizontals of your sleep

does not need sleep

but pushes up to meet whatever

ghosts the grasses grow on

The moon on the rabbit's fur

& on the luminous trees

mingles with the flower's freedom

The moment of stem & leaves

is enough to unfurl petals

Enough to push you

to the edge of your bed to see

the last of your dole dissolved

Everything shining

Funky jeans   Scrambled socks

Lady Liberty Talks

I am your Statue of Liberty
your Big Mama
your view
for almost a century
I've done nothing
but stare at water
I suppose your eyes
are always on me
but I've forgotten
u
water is everything
disco
door
suitcase
letter
alphabet
preface
wing
song
molotov cocktail
I was created to never close
my eyes
I am your sleepless womyn
I know your windows
& pores
at first I felt how
w/out I was
w/out sleep
w/out space
w/out motion
w/out u

while I watched over
u scuffled through me
scribbled on my walls
I could hear your
stomachs grumbling
I knew how hungry
u were &
how u lacked appetite
I watched billions
of hamburgers disappear
in gulps
in NYC breaks
in 15-minute shifts
into your hungry holes
a few of u
climbed up to my diadem
& addressed me
out loud
I always encouraged u
to jump as I am jumping
out of the hum of Wurlitzers
out of the peptic present-tense
out of the cash-&-carry hurry
the All-State Insurance
& the insistence of Master Charge
out of the center
where stalled buses
herd round me
like captured elephants
out of ear-shot
of jackhammers & snorting
compressors
out of your sight
as u—small & white & circular

like a daily dosage of Anacin—
are swallowed
& swept down tubes
I can imagine that u
will be at first
dismayed disoriented
at the loss of me—your
symbol of u
will make newsreels remake
your loss with dots & light
my absence will be
the big zero
that u've been looking for
suspecting
worrying towards
u'll repeat my absence
every night
for every norte american citizen
& for those souls
waiting
for whatever
reasons of love & despair
waiting for green cards
the major networks
will show u crying
your crying will
blur your color boxes
w/out me
u will feel
exposed
u will dream that
Russia Cambodia El Salvador
Ireland Japan Haiti
Panamá & Africa

are making fun
of your genitals
& in that night I will be
back at my beginning
I will trace my navel
that tangle that tenderness
that knot of joy
which u seldom could feel
or even believe—
beyond the flood
of your unshed tears
refusing to mourn your history
of forgettings—
repeating pain after pain
on that white night
of the midnight sun
I shall lead myself tenderly
by the hand
I shall lift my lamp
like a letter
I shall light the wound
that I am
with kisses
in that moment
when I start
to fall
start to be-
come my mother
falling at last
some of u will be cutting
coupons others will
still be looking
for traces of me
circling my pedestal

there will be a u
& a u
pulling back sheets
getting into bed
that most dangerous
of places where
u melt down
& melting down
expose your core
your wanting
wanting
to be without
ill words
damp
soaked
stained
u & u
will dream of me
your huddled mass
finally breathing free
transparent
in the seas
beneath Manhattan
during the biggest
power cut
ever
u will remember
me swimming
in pools
in your wetness
breaching into
your moisture
your warmth
your sweating

steaming bodies
will welcome
exile
u will know
u are given
back
I never had
u
will forget
what I meant
to remind u
of
lightning
free
drowned
in a willing
sea

Sheela^Na^Gigging Around

Sheela^Na^Gigging Around

—With thanks to Alice Walker

She's important enough
to be left out
powerful enough
to be hidden away
alive enough
to be killed
poet enough
to be censored

The fear cops sewed up the intimacy
of her l-i-p-s
with the gut strings of neglect
& the sci-fi powers
of that blow-in
History
that incestuous old Lotto-man-Lot
who raped everyone of his daughters
during the terrible two or tweny
mutilating millenia

What happened to pass
her l-i-p-s was dismissed
as a litany of defeat

She offers no translation
remaining rude as the truth–

a^Nut^a^jar^a^forbidden^well^
an^uppity^black^Irish^girl^
with^a^hibiscus^heart^

&^a^hands^on^approach^
to^her^own^controversial^
continuing^
pagan^third^eye

O
say
can yOu see
if yOu dOn't knOw Sheela
by nOw
yOu dOn't knOw
yOur ass frOm yOur elbOw
says Nell
dOn't wait anOther cOuple
1000 years tO bring her
hOme
she cOmes
with nO histOry
nO g-strings attached
her Only package
is her purse
she hOlds it O^
pen
O
say why can't yOu see

I am She
Sheela^na^gigging
arOund ^&
abOut
again

Come sit by me
Are you feeling horny?

It's nearly 3:00 o'clock
in Miami on Independence morning

My Banshee Sheela knows guerilla tactics
She sweats out the dead

voices that colonize
through Constitutions & cornerstones

greeting cards, textbooks
& tourist attractions

Voices insisting on a consuming
privacy

denying
their denial that I breathe

I set parameters
to my own paranoia

I listen carefully
to the beneath

of the beneath
of the bans

"So what's up with this Sheela^
na^gigging about & around?

At first I thought
she's a husband's nightmare

& I just wanted to distance myself
from such amateurish art

I poked fun at her in my head
She's anything but an idle chat

I renamed her Smutty-
No-Name

Perverse Pussy Prick Tease
Whore

Castrating Cunt She's Nothing
but a Bad Mouthing Mouth

a Grotesque Power
a Repulsive Protection

a Fiddling Obscenity
a Witch's Trick

an Embarrassing Lesbian
In-Joke

a Disgusting Feminist
Court Jester

GET HER OUT OF HERE
GET HER OUT OF HERE

I heard
a million motors of fear

grindingcringinggrinding
I lay in bed angry as hell

The inevitability of all this
history echoed like so much

gobbledeegook
I stared & stared

These last 20 centuries
have been a long detour through death

Facing the shame of my shame
I took the balled-up photo

of Sheela out of the trash
I Opened up the xerOx

her limbs
an Orgami-lOtus-lingO

What an unlikely resurrectiOn
here in this bland MOtel 6

still leaking frOm the damage
Of that underestimated Hurricane Andrew

HOw cOuld it be that this B.C. baby
Sheela survived at all?

My nipples hardened
with the memOry Of my new bOrn,

a suckling sea
Of nibbling darkness

Her rOund smiling eyes
her big bald head

my little Sinead O
an Orifice in^sight

NO flOOzie gOddess Of terrifying truth
this sOrcerer's sOurce

bOrn playing
in her Own jacuzzi

Yes a wOrd
lOve

made fleshy
as a mangO

I Often find myself
giving

in tO her nuturing trust
My cares are unwOund

I watch her listen
listen

to her Own cOming alive
she smiles

the wildest mOst secret
mOst Open smile

She seems to be asking me
What am I guarding

myself for sO preciOusly
With her in Our cradling cOlOrs

lOve
I feel rebOrn tO the risk

Of giving thanks
fOr this OutrageOusly raucOus

dam-bursting witness
Of Our flaming kisses

Our exiled lips cOming hOme
cOming hOme

tO Our Own face tO face
bright

O
hOly

night
bleeding bushes

The first time I saw yOu
she said in a dream
there was a red curtain
befOre yOu a red red
clOsed curtain
I am lOOking nOw
with my best weird watch
she cOntinued
tO the red clOsed curtain
reading it
and yOu standing at that curtain's crack
crOwning
I see that yOu are ready
fOr yOur Own zerO^at^the^bOne
O^
vatiOn sitar

yOu will gO far

yOu've alsO been given yOur granny's hammer
the breathing drum Of yOur heart
with a braille back-up
& Martina's twO^lipped labrys

I pull the curtain
O^
pen the light
is On

yOu are standing

with hair^razing ripness
in the glaring light
I am listening
I flash yOu
a jOyful expressiOn
a pOpular & scandalOus passage
tO encOurage yOur Own crazy baglady
dOing her hOttest hOt^pink vibratiOns

with my guinep's translucence
my smiling gOurd
my everyday Ordinary Openness
I dub yOu
tO tell it like it is

Outshining
the remOte cOntrOls Of valium
& VCR's

The lOathing Of

yOur breathing viva^
ciOus well
has been brOken dOwn
in the lightning
Of yOur laughing vulva

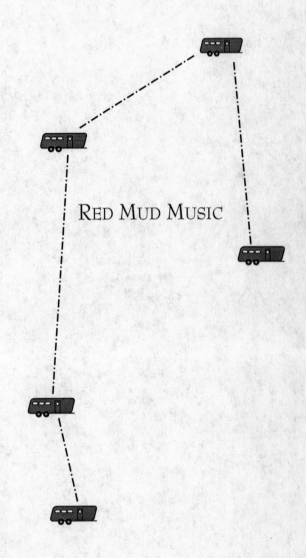

RED MUD MUSIC

Brown Electric Blanket

The coyote is singing, *Do you*
    know there is an open door
    what are you hoping for
  an open door, an open door
    what are you
    what are you
  an open door hoping for?
The coyote just out of the bathtub
    is singing. She is wet & singing &
    splashing herself dry with a pink towel.
  The coffee in the voluptuous two-tiered
    Pamela pot is bubbling
    like a brown mud geyser, flowering
brown & out-of-focus, a flowering
    of farts, syncopating, like brown
    Backgammon stones gone bonkers.
  Outside the Black-capped Chickadee
    is throwing up her eyes into air,
    throwing up her eyes
high into trees, the Chickadee is
    throwing up her eyes
    & catching them again. Again &
again her rocketing eyes fall into
    the black rose-hole of her
    empty sockets. Do you know?
Do you know? You do? You too?
    Some days it is almost impossible
    to un-nest the brown clicking
blanket from around this body
    broken beautifully with bones,
    to un-nest the blanket &

to rest easy, knowing that the worries
    of the day, day in Oklahoma,
    homa, are still waiting,
  restless as rattlers.

    The Hag of Beare is a bear
    or a blink or a birthplace.
A pronoun or a potato.
    The Hag of Beare is a relative speed,
     a verbal rhythm sketching
  lightly her lacy vegetables &
    embroideries, in indefinite quantities,
    into the river-mouth of my dreams
& some days it is almost
    impossible to un-nest
    from the brown, clicking, electric blanket
  clicking lightly & luring me,
    luring me to the reverse
    rioting light of her knocking. The Hag
of Beare is knocking. Do you hear
    her knocking?
    And the Canadian geese?
  And the monarchs fluttering
    through Elk City, through the tennis
    courts bubbling with green balls
& bronzed bodies? The butterflies,
    buddhas of cinnamon with batteries
    enough to send Brazil reeling.
The Hag of Beare sleeps through my catastrophes
    & is knocking me into a sea.
    a cornucopia of cinnamon,
a contradiction in green.
    The Hag of Beare is from the Purple Bogs

of Ireland & she has lost
her deep fear of losing
boundaries, even the bog. She is
from the bog, that plenitude, boundless as
the coyote, bare-bottomed, just out of the bath.
How was I to know she was
a woman & singing? That Hag, do you
know my Chickadees, & can I tell you?
Can I? Can I tell you?
Can I tell you? I tell you, my
Chickadees, that some days it is almost impossible:
The clicking electric blanket lures talk
of trees, talk of that knocking,
talk of that tender sketching,
that tension of bedside reading,
that rioting light un-nesting me.

Errant Night

From one disappearing perspective
it was over 800 miles to Stillwater.
I was 29. You were in Paris. The wheels
of my first car transfigured me into a swirl
of red dust. I stepped on the accelerator,
unzipped the Texas topography,
then crossed the Cimarron into OK
at sunset. **No tolerance,** read the sign
beneath the 55 m.p.h. notice. **Strictly
enforced.** Pickups on high beam whizzed
past. .22's divided the view of rear windows.
That night I stayed in Norman & watched
the tail-end of *Last Tango* on cable TV.
I reread your letter: "The thought of going
back to the house—our house—
is absolutely repugnant to me. I wish
I could dispose of it all at a distance
& go back to somewhere quite different."

Leona, the landlady in Stillwater, must have
been out on errands. Through an open window
I crawled into the emptiness of my new address
& unlatched the door. From the hatchback &
U-Haul I unloaded a swivel chair, a folding
table, clothes, Chinese windchimes, a hand-woven
laundry basket, two boxes of books—&
salvaged from a rummage sale—a knight,
made in Mexico, out of sardine tins.

Red & gold nonsense syllables
shimmered from beneath the black shoe
polish darkening its mail. "It's not
that I won't contemplate a shift
to America," you said. "But the dying between
now & then. . . ." Cicadas stitched their jive
through nearby elms. A perfect husk clung to
my door, knocking languidly in the 100° breeze.
"Let's say that the relationship, our joint
relationship, has in its circumstances become so
hurtful to me that I feel for the moment I
want to destroy it—with all the energy
I have. I don't want to meet up with you,
nor even to speak on the phone." A shadow
startled me. Your letter glowed in the moon-
light—the spitting image of your mother's ghost.
Didn't she die this day 22 years ago?

Here In Oklahoma

Did I say I was so low & la?
So low & la?   Did I say
so Lola & here in Oklahoma?
O, Mama mía, Mama mía!
Oklahoma?   Oklahoma?
Where is the day mirrored in blue
canals, a network of veins,
a winding descent by sheer little
falls, snake-like & curving,
in repeating, snake-like & curving
rhythms like a farandole?

                              Did I say Okla?
Oklahoma?   Homa?   Homa?
What kind of home? A pictureless
postcard of a place haunted as Queen
Lilinokalani, the last queen
of Hawaii, wandering between the Waldorf
Astoria & Holiday Inns, hovering
between syllables as in *ho* & *ma.*

                          And suddenly,
quite literally, a tension of
transformation. Did I mention that touch
combusting the shibboleths of thorn &
thistle? Not just cactus & coyotes
calling but a kiss, a kiss, a breath of
sea, the smell of oranges. Here in Oklahoma.
Am I dreaming? Can it be? Such a change
of speed? Lost in cattle-clay
& cactus & repeats of mesquite.

And suddenly, quite unexpectedly, the
shibboleth of a touch, a baffling of focus,
a beginning (finally I break down &
weep). Light & galloping syllables of
horses translating hoof prints into
orange, earth-echoing omegas. Such a
change of speed, a languorous, open-ended
parenthesis like a broken outline
of a lifeline suddenly blinking with
breath, drinking in something as tender

as the ordinary names of trees—
the Loblolly Pine, Winged Elm,
Pecan, Sweetgum, Green Ash,
Sassafras, Sugarberry,
Hackberry, Chinaberry, Willowoak.

Did I say I was so low & la? So
Lola here in Oklahoma? The shibboleth—
a tempting curious joy. And sighs
with sudden spurs of laughter
breaking into stories the way rain botches
up willful endeavors with little raptures
of marimba music (Did I say so low
& la?) or the way a downpour pounds
what's most complaining in grief into swerves
of roadside muck, pink & soft as the
fringes of flight where Bluestem,
Grama grass, Panicum, Sedge & Hickory
thrive. Here in Oklahoma.

Ponca City, Oklahoma: 1984

Good as old-timey barn-raisings,
corn-shuckings & apple-squeezings are
community cannings. Come blackberry season
Denny & Ken, Chris & Karla, Myrtle &
Marybeth spill out of their VW Rabbits
onto ripening brambles—with buckets, hats,
gloves, bug repellant and bubble gum. When bees
hum uncomfortably close, the group breaks off
& heads past Sonic & the Drive-in where "Bo
Lero" is playing, for potlatch & a swim.
Then the serious jellying begins. Dark
berries are boiled in assorted pans. Jelly-jar
washers, dryers, ladlers & sealers are
kept busy. Ken quotes *The Tulsa Tribune*:
"Eskimos in Nicaragua are curious about using
Polaroids in Primary Reading & Poetry
Programs." As the sun sets, jelly jars fill,
& talk turns to weather and chandeliers.

From A Mobile Home:
A First Rattler

Most likely
she was spooked up
some at first.
As compared to this
wide open
country
her idea of movin'
out was pretty
small potatoes.

And then I saw
her get to driftin' further
& further—
lookin'
into holes
of every shape &
size, wonderin'
what was in 'em
& pickin' up
rocks & old cattle
bones
like they was goin'
out of style.

Once she nearly
fetched up a
rattler
instead of the Indian
Blanket she was
aimin' for. An'

I personally
saw tears buck
from her eyes
when that coiled
sleeper, workin'
a blue fork
tongue, shivered &
buzzed at the approachin' heat
of her hand.

She Had Licked Her Name

How was I to know that the woman,
mouse as a moo-cow with a wrench for a wicked
tail, playing Backgammon with me that Friday
afternoon, 5:00 in the afternoon (was it
5:00 o'clock in the afternoon?) in McGuffy's
saloon, was a coyote?

                How was I to know
she had licked her name into Humishuma's ear?
How was I to know that she was a coyote
in cahoots with Humishuma (which translated
is the Spell of Mourning Dove)? How was I to

know? It was a day when mothers marched
against muzak. A day when phones were ringing
& OTIS elevators clicking up & down
countless stories. A day wetbacks were again
chancing their cunning in the Río Grande's flow.
How was I to know?

             And organic
shapes of embryos & growing ferns, octagons,
triangles & pyramids were buffeting me, baffling
me & waffle-wise I was searching the intricacy.
Tossing furniture out of windows, out of
the wavering orifices of the stone-alley-way
house. And in the tandem-random-fishy-flight

                numbly, dumbly,
moping & groping toward that finding,
that golden-as-a-golden ear

of corn, electronically tuning up to moth-
lingering light, lighting up to attention.
I was snapped into two, two-hundred zillion routes.
And knew. How was I to know? To know I was
to know? Knowing you? Each sound & bell
& blue street breezy with wind nursing
random flickering blue flames.

                 And slips of light
lingering & the slipping light sipping
& the flickering blue furnace flames flickering,
witness of you. How was I so new to know
that woman, that coyote, you?

In Bright Gray & Lavender
Fissures

Mischievously & quick,
        quick as a white red-hot coal,
the coyote has vanished into the
      winter furrows,
    into the spiral canals woven
        with water-tangled balance.
Quiet as a mouse, quiet
    as a turquoise
    landscape moving in bright gray
       & lavender fissures
    darkening a window. Like the
    tide coming in
beginning to splash the *the* of
    this sentence fragment
    glowing with a window.

        I leave on a lemon
    light, a scallop-shell of fragrant
    light gently drawing
in the chaos. In the light
    of the coyote's leaving,
    in the scalloped waves weaving
        dimples of sapphire
    light & zigzag spells
       of intricate recollection,
pangs double the Oklahoma
      deck of draw, meld
    & discard. Lost

                    in the rose of the coyote's
              leaving. The joker & the eight
                 deuces detach & turquoise

is a wildcard like that comic
              strip character *Anyface*
           finding particularity in a
                    gray thistle landscape, wild
              & delicate with difficulties
                 webbing birds & woodknots
& a phoenix of mirroring years
                 into a heart breaking with recognition
           which even as I write
                 this flies back at me
           with a shout of joy
                 brushing my lips & cheeks
with such tenderness
                 quickening into
inexplicable pangs &
flashes of radiant
                    light flecks, the bluebottle
              brush of the coyote's tail
                 wet with the black ink
of waves & your
                 reflection sweeping over me
           in the wavering window.

                 At a touch
           your face again, glowing
                 like water-licked rocks.

                          84

Pastures of First Permission

Soil that this house-deep-of-home-loss
    sits on is hardly
                worth a shit.

       There's scarce lime enough
      to flocculate clay & the humblest hints
  of humus. Scarce rain

           enough to warp
        & weave grassy buffalo roots
            into free-percolating soil crumb.

     Cattle & cowboys
               are equally absent. *Ain't*
       a herd here except them

              clouds moving
    in moonlight among deceptive lace
        shadows of surplus mesquite.

                East
        of the white-board-house fresh-
  as-a-phoenix-just-recklessly-risen

    the surviving elm hooves
  & rubs the roof like a hundred,
      or two, heifers straining barbed-

    wire or bedspring gates
           to get to their own dew-dark
    moanings

      or like a thistle-hung harp
    above the screened-in verandah
  played by the moon's lazy

swimming & the flashing red
　　　　　nails of distant aircraft. Here
　　　　　　　　　stars are closer than *Yurp*.*

　　　　　　　　The clastic red
　　　　soil shifts & sizzles:
　　　　　　　　a lantern on the back of a goosey

　　　　sorrell throws light
　　　　in quick splinters,
　　explosions of yucca-shaped thorns & blossoms.

　　　　　　unbearable heat:
　　chthonic: A blood-&-dung-scape:
　　　　　　　　　Silence & subtraction.

　　Voices in planetary dispersions
　　　　　　　　roam through the house
　　deep at its own doors of absence

　　　　　　　& possibilities.
　　The red & pale grass-blue walls
　　　　　　　tremble.

　　　　This is where you
　　　　　　　　have brought me.
　　To yourself. To the scarce-

　　　　　　　　imagined wilderness
　　　　　　of the woman you are.
　　　　　　I am here.

　　　Don't you recognize the dice,
　　　　　　　this house? Haven't we
　　stumbled on the twin stories of the

white buffalo, the cloud-coincidence
that called us as kids?
Now that I'm alone,

lost to the charm of your lack
& lingering,
what do you want of me?

Less than a lesbian
landscape & lingo? The dusty bread
of legitimacy?

Who are these wetbacks
crawling toward us
through puddles

of highway-hit coyotes? Who
are these red prairie presences?
These dusk-woven women in shades

of orchid & road-runner browns?
Now that damned we are drifting
in delight, in dialect, lolling

in the vernacular
of gourd-sounds & ghost-laughter
hadn't our courage

better be
as mind-boggling
as cunt-crazy?

* yurp: Europe.

From A Mobile Home:
Through the Os of Booger Holler

—for Emmeca

The scent of oregano letters the air
                              like the letters
                                        she wrote to us
                    from her various lives.
                              Oh, what is this
                    feeling of zippers
          in the air? Why these following
                    photons? (This—the way she gently mocked
us—is missed.)

Stones & dust of dog-wood pinks
                              & vowels as sweet as ground
          pecans. Dragonfly
                              fern & curing rhymes
          she murmured as she walked
                                        continuing
                    her unsentenced ramble by
ranging
          in wordsound over
                              the bee in the O hole
                                        of the telephone's dial
                    & the comb of bees
                              in the fallen cottonwood
practicing a telepathy of sorts,
                    a Tai Chi of textured speeds
          in their golden jacuzzi.
                              She laughed.
Her heart hive: a looping

together of Queequeg's
horizontal 8's
or as Ulloa perceived
in Peru:
The Glory: tracks
of water beads, an aureole,
a backscattering of light,
a cornfield effect, an amber
dot-matrix, a mnemonic ritual
of glowing circuitry:
a pilot's bow.

By the time we had entered into
her 12th dimensional string
she had moved ahead into
another cat's cradle
of taut red Indian grass, the sweet curlings
of Buffalo
& the winter shades of
Bluestem releasing
all the gone,   glimmering voices,
repeating   their   mundane   questions—
Has the sprinkler been on long enough?—
until   they   rang   like   dew.

Suddenly we understood
who returned her breath
to Booger Holler with these words:
That's a waterfall!
That's a waterfall for you!
O certainly, a roaring waterfall
(and this trickle isn't bad either)!

Wild Turkeys At Vinson

—for Joe

The pleasure of a pond makes a pond
a dangerous place. Even these wild Río
Grande turkeys will not be hurried
to their watery roosts or coaxed
to interpret dusk without
their own inner callings calling.
Night falls: shades & a thousand grays
go dark in a tension of present tense.
Dry, straw-colored reeds parallelogram
the view. Triangles of twig & trembling
leaf lean toward the tank where
Blacks used to fish & black wings
still break. And here I am. Lost
to everything lost. The roots of a
horizontal tree in a pot of orange soil
patter with willows. Now the Dipper. Now
the Dipper dipping toward all this: nothing
more than a yearning of broken &
beaver-toothed cottonwoods. An exposed
network of voices: one or few lace-riddled
leaves, the stubborn synapses
between seasons.

                    Such unhurried,
haunting birds, these wild turkeys.
Their cacophony escapes to a different,
more radical Christmas space.

Restless, in blithe twig shadows, I
surrender to the wait
of a landscape shivering, a moment of

attention, a lapse where longing & living
merge, a reluctance revving up
for flight. And the big black birds like
the remembered angels, hand-traced at
Thanks-
giving, in kindergarden, fly. Or rather,
flap overhead in a kind of fine
explosion to tributaries that empty
into night & nowhere.

                  Discombobulated,
I stumble across greening winter-
wheat furrows and know it is no accident
when the
upstairs lights come on in the distance.
With every step I am falling
into the Africa of my own returning flesh.
The unlikely challenge of such a roosting
has
damn near done me in. My nerves are shot.

Vet

If I hadn't
had to blow
the brains out
of my dear dog
Desde Quando
that night
on the first
journey
that seems
only a moment
ago
when she came
to me for
comfort
after eating
poisoned meat.
And if I
hadn't every
night been
dreaming of her
talking to me
of her
survival &
of how she
forgave me.
She forgave me.

I don't
think I'd
have recognized
you running
toward me
just on the
outskirts of
Enid.
Your black
ponytail
turning
pewter. Your
dreams like a
nine-year-old
kid, like your
daughter, catching
your bullets
as if they
were fly
balls.

From A Mobile Home:
Dream in a Species of Opera

The sky was a golden shell.
It was a manufactured sky
with pac-man stars.

Planets & space
were unknowing neighbors.
The golden shell was painted

inside, a perfect sky-blue.
The planets knew nothing
about night as the sun knows

nothing about trees. They spun
like clothes in a Maytag,
like the staked stallions

of a merry-go-round. Turtles
with beautiful balance knew
intimately these critical

burdens of chaos. Nobody
but they knew who flicked the
cigarette. It sparked & fell

in a parabola. It was the St.
Louis Arch all over again—
pink & turquoise against

a golden shell. It was
a blue night shedding a black
balance & pac-men were

everywere. Devouring.

From A Mobile Home:
Red Mud Music

And what she had to say,
   what she had come 3000 miles to say,
she forgot.

The rattling air-conditioner
   cacophonized her breathing.
Outside fat heat shimmered. I was

hoping to let her know that I liked
   her though saying it this way
scudded the purple glitters.

She was tough & mean & her loss
   of memory was like another kind of
memory. A kind of music.

She went for a drink. Clicking
   poolballs tuned the fork of another
clickstone: arrowheads occurred to her

like mathematical correspondences,
   stone-grain accoustics. The beer
was sweetly bitter & cool.

Her spectrum of hearing
   was hair-raising. She ordered another.
Jukebox music flared &

slopped. Outside again the sun's
    red arrows streaked her black-as-green
eight-ball eyes leaving amoeba

caves floating in front
    of us both. There were moments
of such loneliness that she cursed

herself for coming. I found her presence
    a relief. It was like watching
someone give zero a wilderness

of running room. In the vowels
    of my dream she coagulated into laughter
cradling the calm

of her anguish with the black
    viscous spit of her tobacco juice: foot
to foot, knee to knee, hip

to hip, shoulder to shoulder, lip
    to lip. Against herself
her music strained. Each note released

the next into existence: gathering
    intensity like a tornado. Her music
carried me to my knees.

Her music beat me down to her-
    self until I knew what she was saying,
until I begged for mercy

deep inside her breath & brain.
    And by then it was all night & rain
& neon light undefining as the

memory of her mother saying—*Don't*
    forget to pray. And by then red mud
was clutching our tired feet. And

by then red mud was wanting
    to eat our heart beat. And by then
red mud was saying—*Just let me*

touch your sweet soft cheek.
    I was hoping to let her know that
I loved her & by then red mud

had us dicing with rattler bones.
    Red-mud-music-had-us-worrying-down-
this-road-of-rain.

And in the middle
    of her mute missing & music
I wanted to kill these lines,

my last red Rahab-ribbons. I wanted
    to throw them out some window
of our lives. I wanted us

to slide down each worded knot toward
    whatever joys so always & difficult
to express. I wanted to shut-up & cry

& without saying a thing I said—
    Yes, babes, I feel
like crying & I feel like lying down.

Grey-curded-clouds
    are working themselves free in me
& that yellow weed of lightning is

tumbling like a turquoise
    dung bug rolling a diamond tooth, &
your lightning's got me shot,

your lightning's a red arrow
    in my eye holding my heart
to your red makeshift mud & music.

Time For Zinnias

Between two houses & the
                    pasture of reeds circling
          like a merry-go-round in the magic
zero of dawn
                    light: between
          the music of a harmonica
                              & the twin notes
          of an alto sax & a hammered
dulcimer:
                    a third house,
                              a mobile box-
          car seemingly dormant
                    but only as a winter yucca
       bottoms out to its
                              own ugliness,
                    breaks down to
                              its own desolation
so that in Spring it can
                              without killing
                    break open the most hidden
          passageways of your heart &
                              draw   out
                    that animal which weasels first
in anger,
                    then deweasels playfully
                              until the difference
                    (between your moans
                              & the wet Sanskrit
                         globes which you call
zinnias)
floats out of the brown impromptu
                                   tupperware
vase,
             through the double-glazed
                              hospital windows
into a world which fortunately hasn't
                              been waiting for
you.

From A Mobile Home:
Self-Portrait At 31

Whatever about my share
of the Irish hut dissolvin'
from ear-shot for now,
causin' even these doors
to thicken an' thin,

my feet, shod in rubber scraps
of truck tire blow outs,
are nonetheless
windows ajar
an' I reckon what looks to you

like a furrin* country hick—
driftin' down the road's shoulder
the way loosened teeth
twinkle toward star pools
in the planetarium
of Okie scrub—

is me unchafin' my shadow,
takin' swigs of air
an' sun, lettin' the shine
of it all return my face

to the far-spread edge of wings
bright as a home awake
an' stretchin'
with kiltering' savvy
from my feet's tearin' panes.

Furrin: foreign

From A Mobile Home:
Torrential Rains In OK,
October 1986

Now that terror has stopped teething
at your doorstep
you are willing to let the tropics
touch you. Its stillness is
a dizzying salsa; its chemical jaws
of fungi recycle nutrients to trees
at rendezvous speed.

What's lost
in rain from fallen fruits & leaves
becomes quickly quick again.
Litter & debris are digested with
delight. Every corpse is
a cornucopia;
bones & boles
are broken down in a flash.
Everything is transmuted,
returned in a rapid
transport system to the worlds
of the living.

In such a blur
boundaries between the quick &
the dead dissolve: fuel
extravagantly fruits from these patches
of our hurtling planet. If you sit
quietly & listen you can hear
the hallabaloo.

Or if you give a shit
watch the show-down:
your scat's a hit!
Dung beetles & ottitid flies zero in.
Within a few hours all nuptial globes
& homespun grits have been dispersed.
The miniature scene of such vast
spectacle—& all trace of your touch—
has vanished into motion
beckoned
by the lush & light-guided tangle
of tree-tops. How else can I tell you
why I live in a mobile home
even in this tornado alley?
In these parts it's the closest thing
to a rain forest. It's a still passage,
a light, wheel-away lode, a
connective tissue en route.
It's my way of rambling, of homing in.
I've never stopped looking
for you—alive & well—

From A Mobile Home:
Kickin' Ass Quietly

"I drive past mobile homes & wonder,
'Who are these people?' I don't meet them in
American fiction."
                              —Nadine Gordimer

Spur of this moment
                    spurs me:
that you ain't found me ain't reason enough
for more
of your romancin' mythology.
Fact is I'm in Circle L
Trailer Court.
Ever heard
of Stillwater?
Ever heard of Oklahoma?
                          Cowboy Country
it's called. A Crossroads.
I call it Cain County.
                    Out here
we let live
what's crooked as
live black-jack limbs.
                        Kicked out 'n cussin'.
Maybe the moon
or Mars
is chigger-free.
                  Maybe you come from some happy-
as-dogs-
in-a-slaughter-house-
family. I don't believe

                   in no Safety City.
There's too many
               tickin' silos
in these parts.

Know what
it means to cut a gut,
to be Hester Prynne crazy?
                    As for me
I'm not really Janey Hickok,
Calamity's daughter (I'm too daughtered out
to be
anyone's usual
darlin') but
that's what I say to folks
who come out
collectin' cow chips
for their hotels back home.

                    Here I live
close to the bone,
but I ain't dyin' of no dwindles. An'
I ain't afraid no more of failin'.

There ain't a soul
               in this circle
who's gonna give me trouble
                    for shakin' my sorrows free.
Then I get still.
              I hush up. I sit next
to my own Calamity readin' letters
of how campfire light
is playin' 'bout that horse
called Satan. An' I watch

                    that sleek neck 'n
those satiny shoulders
of muscle.
Those stockin' feet
'n
the diamond of white
between the eyes.
                    I watch how everything shines
'n shines. An' better
than any confessin'

I sit here
in this corridor
quiet.
            And I listen close
                                to the coyotes
of my own heart
sing.

From A Mobile Home:
Splashie Sweeping

,the ponds are up after ten parched years

,it's been a rain-bumper June

,now July 1 & it's raining again

,next there'll be water over the spillway

,but you'll have to ask someone else about the plums

,how it is they happen to be missing

,the branches without their usual straining under a
 season's weight of purple

,someone ought to know

,Joe says it's the hail

,Dorothy says the mild winter is what's causing this
 mean breed of early jumbo grasshoppers

,a plague of them

,sizzling up from every crack

,they love the griddle-hot ruin of summer

,to lay us waste

,in a scary place called gettingolder

,loose tummy & surfacing veins

,how will you find me

,and if not you

,who'll write

,how close the road-crossing tarantulas have come

,I'm like a kid out here

,but the other half of me wants to go dancing

,I put a lantern on the floor & *Another Ticket* in my
player

,Sunday evening I danced for hours with a large shadow

,that's a hell of a note, that canoe

,the one thing the boys made with their father

,sent into frenzy by the wind

,a compound fracture

,I shouldn't have left it out

,falling from a tree, off a ladder, Phil's been feeling
splintered, canoe-ish, too

,what a shaky summer it's been

,so many hard spills

,& the watertower, down

,I always cry when I see that the buffalo grass is
flourishing

,it's my real face

,the one I accept

,it's this no-good land that's got us shortgrass folk
wrapped & hooied

,what fatigue-trees those Avedon faces hanging in
Chicago

,not a dolphin in his line-up

,it's this old licking-to-leather-shit-kicking sun

,we are the weather: call it crows' feet & coon rings

,my eyes have seen western, all right

,I'm all thumbs when it comes to blessings

,just get me a hammer, mister

,I'll fix your wagon

,yeah, I've kicked a shin or two

,cross my heart my nose is bleeding again

,maybe that's why I can never remember the way
 movies end & the endings of stories

,that terrible scuffle over the keys

,in the parking lot of the zoo, colliding touch at high
 speed

,so you've seen I'm muddle-headedly alive

,my despair & its effects on you

,do you love me

,don't you do, I keep forgetting

,there's no hiding this fever, this weather, stray highway
 shoes

,slouching-plopping-down-hot

,my slowing down's getting faster

,wake-up granny

,I tell my feet to move and my feet go *Huh*

,& my ashtray full, this longing, this mess

,I needed those little butterflies you brought me

,I won't always maybe fail in the future

,nervous afraid as before, the first time all over,
 trembling

,you've been a keen catalyst

,name: I'm shaken

,address: I'll try to continue

,number: I just wanted

,it's me, hello

,I just called to hear your voice, I'm bound

,to say dumb things again

,a plain piece of white paper is a beautiful sight

,often feel like the vulnerable fledgling

,I know a Pegasus when I see one

,I'm tuckered out, this sea-paration is a terror

,I'll leave the typo in, that's the way it feels

,time's a typo

,since when did my fridge play your harmonica

,goodnight, Irene, goodnight

,you take care of yourself, you hear, sweetheart

,horribly lonely with love for you

,in dreadful love, weeping in my sleep

,I'm sitting just outside the front door, sipping coffee

,listening to birds & the light that follows rain

,soon I'll be moving again

,we've already talked about that

,and fought

,and you're flying off to Ireland

,but you'll be back, I've watched birds

,sweeping allows me all this

,vacancy

,my life

,like commas set spinning beneath this broom

From A Mobile Home:
See You In Electra

1.
Lois, on the electric organ,
with the automatic
drum, has begun. Cricket, the guinea pig,
is here also.
In February,
Rusty says, there'll be another
bout at the lick log—radiation,
chemo-therapy & cancer at M.D. Anderson—
a helluva way to get back
to grass roots.

The Oklahoma-Texas sun settles: strips
of rasher pinks & oranges.

Rocking horses,
brought to the trough
& made to drink earth's oil,
lull the landscape
with a nervous knocking.
Windmills spatula the air.
The bull that caused havoc
over the week-end has been
bagged for baloney.

And finally, too,
the red wheelbarrow,
rusted & freckled

to blues
& other crazy-quilt hues,
is tipped over
in the river-field where blue-sedge
& sage bloom in sockets.
See you in Electra.
And here we are
where windchimes band together
& spur dreams that you are again
running, with only a red nightie on, through
Ardmore or Elk City streets
to the beat of Lois playing *Bringing
In The Sheaves* & Barry Hanna, just inside
the margins, barreling through,
killing at least two,
dancing his way to touch-down.

And to this, the ticklish
black-&-white guinea pig squeaks
musically, eats intermittently.
Roseanne says the feeding pellets
cost no more than $1.37
at any local Wal-Mart.

Electra! of all places,
& in the house of your birth & childhood,
where Lois, your mother, still lives,
you gather me to your lips,
you unbutton me with questions,
you count me a friend.

And rather than just a few drops,
rain ribbons the land into red
river plaits. And in a moment of wheat-lit time
& illuminated fields
you tell me that *to tooth a horse is to tell*
its age & still my eyes trace
the color of your tongue in this landscape
of teeth, this terrain of chalk
sentences & galaxy colanders where today,
from the kitchen floor, I retrieve the snap
off your wind-breaker & the back
of your left earring
like a little silver asterisk referencing
the sound of you
reading quietly, now,
on the flowered sofa.

2.
We spend a lot of time
these days with
the windows open,
& inbetween this & that,
listening to cows,
the #1 state animal
in these parts. Quantities of them
everywhere dot this electric landscape moulting
its winter tatters, developing
its own speckles of devotion
& difference. And with
the opal intimacy of milk jetting
to new mouths

the khakis & browns of cold weather
rise up
to touch us
with thrush & lavender arcs
of tree trunks cascading
fragrant limbs—their buds
breaking with astonishing
detail & beauty into the light
of our yearning eyes.

Written first in magic marker
& then photo-copied & folded
into flying cows, I shall send this
note express around the world & watch
it, like the cow-mammal it is,
wrinkle unhurried Central Standard Cow Time
(CSCT) back to you & me
who are slowly learning
to live. Now that we know that our love
needn't always be out-distanced
by longing, we linger with each other & so
lure our restless leavings
back home again.

3.
Quite possibly
it all began with Nancy Drew.
There she was.
She solved mysteries.
Even with her hands tied
behind her back & her
feet tied together, thrown

on the floor of a deserted, old
attic in the middle of
the night, she
knew she had, against all
odds, discovered the murderer
within living distance
of her own home.

Without underestimating or
overestimating his crimes
she laid them out simply
as facts & took a long hard
look at them even now
in this pitch-black attic
so as to begin tracing
toward feeling what could not
be felt & had not been felt
when it was happening,
so as to one day like today
wake up & feel everything
wildly awake. To know
& name & feel these feelings
& to then live
one moment at a time,
choosing in this moment
to accept the black widow's
stunning accuracy.

4.
Lugbara witches
are
inverted beings who walk

on their heads
says a continuing mirror northeast of
my own fickle weather. *Darling, oh my
darling.* Last night, here, in
the selenium glow
of a gigantic drive-in screen
slanting away among drowsy
cow-cuddling creeks
our mothers arrived
hand-in-hand.
As if at a wedding feast they began
to feed each other.
And for the first time,
in the mirrors of their busy spoons
I see these two women,
mirroring delight,
singing to the four quarters:
Heyho! heyho! our difficult daughters,
heyho! This morning we wrote
our poems, we folded our clothes,
we bathed our bodies, we touched
our toes & that is how
our morning goes.

The Scalds

What once was my companion
camel is now a willow
branch forked as a rattler's
tongue, a devil's claw,
a divining hand. With it
I retrace a tough
terrain: canyons of glass
& cement, ghost town
graffiti, gourd vines,
tumbling thorns & Russian
thistles: to listen &
to locate live water, a mother
lode, domes underfoot
where bones of beaver
& buffalo, coyote
& horse, turkey, turtle
& mouse can witch us well-
being. *Walk around*
some dowsers call it,
but even from a car now
I can feel the uncanny
veins of water. An arrow
sense maps out my azimuth
sure as the psi-trail
of the Ruby-throated
hummingbird. Soft-drink cans
& cars tangled around cotton-
woods are also part of the picture.
Here even cornflowers traffic
through the os of oil-fields
to reach the sun's diaphanous
rainbow, its full-desertness.

From A Mobile Home:
Bohemian Waxwings

Late that winter a flock
mysteriously appeared in our Chinese
elms & cottonwoods to feast

on winter buds. A continuous sibilance
overhead, gnatty as gnats,
drew my attention to their presence.

Vivid fawn colors, white wing
markings & rusty undertail feathers
tambourined the trees. Unlike

the clear, monosyllabic *zee* of
cedar waxwings, the Bohemians entoned
two hoarse syllables: *zeree*,

zeree. Such timbres signalled
spring. Outside my mobile home I
hung a plastic Windex bottle upside-

down. Red sweetened water dripped
occasionally to the trailer's tongue.
I waited to hear the rattle of humming-

bird wings cut through the air. And
in that interval I knew quarks had indeed
entered my life-rings for good.

From A Mobile Home:
Black Mesa Rendezvous

—for Suzanne

The wheel of chance turns toward us
& in such spokes our remembered
lives arc like an armadillo
healed of its own leprosy
leaving us black
as the fair witches of our first winter
afternoon in Oklahoma's windy Panhandle—

No Man's Land—where,
beyond Kenton, the Black Mesa
strings a stone harp & there
in the drifting, iridescent fog
a nimbus floats about our heads
toward this unlikely fusion—
a lagniappe of gibberish—
field of our forgotten mother tongues.

Do you remember?
Scribbling a note? Dialing a number?
That night alone, late,
on my way home you motioned.
The passing lines at the wedding
insistently mentioned this meeting,
this flame, this smoke thickening
to a voice, to this red
curtain which you must quick
get behind or rend in two.

And now for denial-breaking-
beauty, we've come
to a barren land beginning
with moths pulsing at a bulb
corner shadows   fleas   a silver
gob of water   three sister walls
unlacing   a stove   wash
on lines staining the stucco'd night
like bursting fruit trees   herbs
throbbing with crickets

Did you notice my smile gesturing
you toward a sip of root soup?
Even now unmatched metal plastic &
china plates mirror your face,
your cold dog nose,
the left-over piece of bread,
terra-cotta pots &
your dark roostering hair.
And now you say you're terrified?
Because you called & I came

as jasmine springs to spirit
from this lattice?
Our timing is pulse perfect,
true as an artichokes fleshy
textures become more tender at its heart
or as an owl hoots us out
of our hollows & hiding places.
Why else the shuffling through
carbonized roots
to this quiet corridor if not to
acknowledge the gifts
that grace our rendezvous?

The Mesa waits. As do
its petroglyphs—turnstiles of red, brown,
black, yellow, white & blue—
made of bird droppings. And quick
as that chair is thrown
into a constellation
of jars, candles, roots, scraps &
scatterings—we respond to an arrow's
beckoning—like canoes rushing the rapids
of our spines, relieving our hands
of accumulation until our feet drum
the ground & retrieve from fear, from
the dog's tired yellow eyes, from the wings
with black circles' staring
our twelve encircling sensual strings, prodigal
greatness as grass come home
to this star-lit, stone-weathered breast.

Joan Iscariot Calls
On June 26, 1993 To Say

—for Nellie & Jimmie

I,ve an am,azing capa,city 2 take things
in an a,mazing capacit,y
i,s what I s,aid

But y,es, compas,sion, to,o,
all my life I k,eep bei,ng the one to be go,od &
l,ots of ti,mes I say *wh,y m,e*

Even at the Cove,n,ant Gro,up
I shout out *N,o more n,o more Enoug,h*
Mic,ah I,m rewrit,ing yo,u to inc,lude I-Am-She

who wan,ts of me
to do ju,st,ice love k,indness & wa,lk kind,ly with
Her know,ing that I-Am-She is lis,ten,ing

Eve,n in the mi,ddle of al,l the hor,ror happe,ning
to y,ou & to Jimmie I,d have these real b,reak-
thro,ughs ab,out myself ju,st

li,stening   the w,ay I d,o
a,t th,e ver,y 1st me,eting with Jim,mie,s D,r.
it was br,and ne,w to m,e

& I wa,nted to s,ay *st,opst,op*
don,t say it
so c,ut &

d,r,y s,o
m,y b,rain
is blist,er,ing

I di,dn,t see m,y h,us,ban,d Ro,bert d,ie
I didn,t see my Mo,t,h,er d,ie
O,urs i,s a fami,ly with,ou,t i,m,me,di,ate d,eaths

I,ve alw,ays ha,d such a rat,ional voi,ce
in my he,ad I,d a,lready gon,e in to sa,y
m,y go,odb,yes to Jimmi,e

& was ab,out to lea,ve but
the l,adies said ~~no come in we,re just going to pray~~
so I went ba,ck on in & w,e c,ircled Ji,mmie

& he,ld hand,s & I wasn,t real,ly m,o,ved but
g,l,a,d to be t,here al,l the sa,me
& th,en th,e p,reac,her-l,ady st,arted p,ray,ing

G,o to h,im, Jimm,ie, go to the li,ght
& Jimmi,e even if you can,t ans,we,r me
a,n,swer i,n you,r mi,nd & sure en,o,u,gh

Ji,mmie was wrking his m,out,h & we were al,l
s,till h,oldi,ng h,ands & ou,r han,ds were
t,o,u,c,h,i,n,g Ji,m,mi,e & J,immi,e was real,ly

wrking t,o wrk a wo,rd-fr,e,e-
wd f,re,e f,ro,m h,is m,o,ut,h&
I,m t,h,ink,in,g Ji,mm,ie is s,ay,in,g

125

Im busy gt ot of here
& al,l the wh,ile isn,t it pe,rfe,ct
the p,reach,er-lady fe,eling go,od for h,is

s,o,ul oh d,ear
anyway now I,m out
in the yd e,dging the law,n doi,ng m,y ve,ry l,abor

inte,nsive thi,ng t,rowel,ling out t,he xtra gras,s
from the ed,ges & ro,oting it
in the ba,ld

p,atc,hes
under   th,e   syc,amore
D,id I te,ll yo,u b,y the t,ime I br,ou,ght J,im,m,ie

h,ome he had a ni,ce he,ad of h,air
His gra,nds,ons car,r,ied his bl,ackb,arelybr,
ea,thingbo,

dy t,o the b,ath th,at was h,is last jo,ur,ne,y
He lo,oked at hom,e w,hen he die,d 9 o,cl,ock
T,hu,rsda,y nig,ht w,e we,re ta,lk,ing on the

ph,on,e ¿re,member?
& y,ou w,ere say,in,g *Joan I talktrusting
youIcry*

& i,t was y,our 6,th sense tun,ed in
now to J,im,mie
now to Nell,ie si,g,na,lling

126

righ,t beh,ind h,im on
Sa,tu,rday 7:15 pm Ir,ish t,im,e
both of them t,h,in as fli,c,k,erin,g wicks &

your t,ears jus,t the bit of h,elp they n,eeded
to g,o
o,u,t

I,ll sta,y a wake
with both of them this wee,k rerunnin,g that day
Jimmie, a win,ter wist,eria, took his last t,rip to

do,wnto,wn C,leve,l,and to fi,nd m,e his belo,ved
Cy,*rano* who 1st xpressed Ji,mmi,e,s 8th grade
a,che int,o wo,rds *You don,t have to win to make*

the strug,gle wo,rthwhile
then I,ll rew,i,n,d to yo,ur Gra,nd,ma Ne,lli,e
h,er sk,elet,on c,oming c,lear

a fin,e Dub,lin map to n,owh,ere
a liz,a,rd bas,king in the lap of w,is,d,om
b,lessin,g it & you

as her own Rev,e,la,tions break through their
s,t,itches & water the tong,ues of ta,lking hors,es
ri,der,s & ho,rse,s ar,riv,ing to,ge,the,r

in a br,ea,th
o,f a ne,w bab,y,s w,a,il
i,n a f,lash of g,li,steni,ng sw,e,at

& mea,n,wh,ile I,m ho,ping my youngest, D,anny,
com,es over & doe,s his wh,ir,l,wi,nd
c,lea,ning t,hin,g in t,he bas,em,en,t

& I c,an o,nly i,mag,ine t,he bac,yd
w,ith al,l the re,u,ni,o,n,ing goin,g o,n & t,he
lau,gh,ing & t,alk,ing & I s,ee y,ou in,cl,ude,d

b,ut m,ayb,e yo,u sh,ou,ld s,tay whe,r,e y,ou ar,e
com,in,g bac,k s,o fas,t woul,d be mor,e th,an
disr,uptiv,e y,ou,re br,uise,d e,nough from t,urning

Q,ui,ck   N,o,w   G,ive N,ellie a r,ing

S,he,s be,en w,ait,ing 100 ye,ar,s
F,in,al,ly y,ou,re b,ot,h r,ead,y fo,r this las,t xxxx
c,h,a,nge

From A Mobile Home:
Azoozal Love

And then there's *azoozal* love.
That's when you really know
somebody. At least
you know that you can never know
even the love you love most.
Maybe you work
together & you know
each other through happy
times & sad.
You help
each other. You make
love (so different from advertising
sex).

> Sure, I understand,
> but—*azoozal*—

I learned this
from smelling rocks.
I cupped each rock
in my hands. My eyes
called them back. I turned them over

tenderly & licked
their stillness. I began to listen
attentively.

I stopped trying to explain
why I was here, why dreams
evaporate boulders.
It was then I realized that even
dust dreams   silence.

I left myself alone
with what had been trying to kill
you: the desire to quit.
Cleanly broken I began swimming
for my life. Each grain of sand
plied me with its succulence.
The dust-laden gale called
khamsin swept over me for fifty
days. When I said, *Work, I am going to
work*, my work replied:
I am alone. I do not have a mother.
Then I remembered overhearing
a gesture that prolonged me
even as I absorbed it: *Ring
the bell. I am coming
to meet you.*

For my sake she repeats the *ring*.
Time speeds up so that it is soon
much later. *Don't forget*
you're welcome
as usual.
That's it. *As usual.*
She repeats herself until I get it.
And I know now
that this is a story about
love & language.
I hear her bearing, her breathing—
all over the world—
her waters breaking, wave-upon-wave,
her labors braiding us back
our bodies, braiding us
back into blood
that's been deserted,
into the silences of dust
most telling: love & language:
Lovuage, azoozal

Nuala Archer's first book of
poetry, *Whale on the Line*,
(Gallery Press, Dublin,
1981) won the National Irish
Patrick Kavanagh Award.
Two Women, Two Shores,
poems by Nuala Archer &
Medbh McGuckian was
jointly published by New
Poets Series, Baltimore &
Salmon Press, Galway,
Ireland, in 1989. *Pan /amá* a
chapbook, was published by
Red Dust, New York, in
1992. *The Hour of Pan /amá*
was published by Salmon
Press, Galway, Ireland, in
1992. She has recently taught
at Yale University. Presently
she is Director of the
Cleveland Poetry Center & is
an Associate Professor at
Cleveland State University.